MONGOLS

Rupert Matthews

W

FRANKLIN WATTS
LONDON · SYDNEY

Franklin Watts

First published in Great Britain in 2016 by The Watts Publishing Group

Copyright © Alix Wood Books
Produced for Franklin Watts by Alix Wood Books www.alixwoodbooks.co.uk

Editor: Eloise Macgregor
Designer: Alix Wood

Photo Credits:
Cover © iStock; 1 background, 3, 9, 10, 11, 13, 14, 15, 21 bottom, 23, 26, 27, 29, 32, 33, 34, 35, 42 © Shutterstock, 1 foreground © Rama; 4 bottom, 22 © Rick Sammon; 7 © Chinneeb; 8 bottom © Fanghong; 8 inset © British Museum; 17 © Tech Museum, San Jose; 18 © U. S. Marine Corps/Sgt. G. S. Thomas; 20 © Enerelt, 21 top © ZhenTianDongDe, 28 © Alix Wood, 31 © Staatsbibliothek Berlin; 38 © junrong/Shutterstock; 41 © kagemusha/Shutterstock; 43 © Brücke-Osteuropa; remaining images are in the public domain

Every attempt has been made to clear copyright. Should there be any inadvertent omission please apply to the publisher for rectification.

ISBN 978 1 4451 5056 7

Printed in China

Franklin Watts
An imprint of
Hachette Children's Group
Part of The Watts Publishing Group
Carmelite House
50 Victoria Embankment
London EC4Y 0DZ

An Hachette UK Company

www.hachette.co.uk
www.franklinwatts.co.uk

Contents

The Mongol empire

The thunder of hooves filled the air, deafening those who heard it. The ground under their feet shivered and shook. Men gripped their swords and fidgeted nervously with their shields as they stared at the oncoming cloud of dust. Then the horsemen burst from the dust. There were thousands of them screaming in anger. The air filled with arrows. The Mongols had come!

The Mongol warriors created the greatest land empire the world has ever known. It was vast, stretching from the Pacific to the Mediterranean, from the Indian Ocean to the Baltic Sea.

Mongol Empire

Speed and power were the secrets of Mongol success. Riding fast horses, the warriors could travel great distances while their enemies were still getting ready for war. Time after time the Mongols would surprise their enemies in this way.

The Mongols planned campaigns carefully. Spies were sent out months or years before a war to learn about the enemy's country and armies. When the Mongols finally attacked they knew exactly where to go and what to do.

A SHORT HISTORY

Although it was large and powerful, the Mongol Empire did not last long. In 1206, the squabbling Mongol tribes united and set out to conquer other territory. After stunning victories, the Mongols began fighting with each other again. In 1368, the Empire collapsed.

Mongol warriors in pursuit.

That's fearless!

The Mongols were ruthless. They killed civilians, women and children. It is thought that 40 million people may have been killed by the Mongols during their conquests! The Mongol conquests may have been the bloodiest wars in all history.

Temujin

It was the Mongol chief Temujin who united the Mongol tribes and created the Mongol Empire. He took the title of Genghis Khan, meaning 'supreme ruler'. The Mongols had been ruled by other powers for centuries. Under Genghis Khan they became rich and powerful.

Genghis Khan

When Genghis Khan was born he was named Temujin by his father, Yesugei, the ruler of the Borjigin clan of Mongols. He was born in his father's tent in about 1155, somewhere near the Burkhan Khaldun Mountain in what is now northern Mongolia. He was born holding a blood clot in his hand, which the Mongols believed meant he would become a great warrior.

AN ARRANGED MARRIAGE

At the age of 16, Temujin married Börte, from the Onggirat tribe. The marriage had been arranged by Temujin's father and the match brought new **allies**. Börte was captured by the Merkit tribe. Temujin set out to rescue her with his friend Jamukha and some followers. After the rescue, Temujin allied himself to the Kerait tribe. Temujin and Börte had four sons: Jochi, Chagatai, Ögedei and Tolui.

When Temujin was nine years old his father was murdered by a gang of **Tatars**. He and his family were thrown out of the Borjigin tribe. In about 1177 Temujin was enslaved by the Tayichi'ud clan. He escaped and built a reputation as a daring warrior, which helped him gain followers.

Temujin and his friend Jamukha became blood brothers, promising eternal friendship. Both men became famous warriors and leaders of several clans and tribes. Eventually they fought each other for leadership of the Mongols. Temujin won.

That's fearless!

Temujin offered to spare Jamukha's life in return for an oath of support. Jamukha refused, saying "As there is room for only one sun in the sky, there is room only for one Mongol lord." He asked to be given a noble death with no blood spilt. His back was broken and he was buried.

The Onon River near Genghis Khan's birthplace

The conquests of Genghis Khan

In 1206, the leaders of the Mongol tribes met and agreed to make Temujin the supreme ruler of the tribes. Once he had united the tribes, Genghis Khan devoted his life to war. China was divided into several separate states. Genghis Khan wanted to conquer them, steal everything, and gain power for the Mongols!

Genghis Khan defeated the **Xi Xia Empire** in 1207. The Xi Xia formed an alliance with the **Jin State**, an enemy of the Mongols. Angry, Genghis Khan invaded and wiped out a Xi Xia army of 300,000 men! Later Emperor Mozhu of the Xi Xia negotiated a peace treaty with Genghis Khan. As he surrendered, Mozhu was killed along with all his men and everyone in the Xi Xia capital of Yinchuan!

A mosque in modern-day Yinchuan

ANNOYING TAXES

In 1211 an **envoy** from the powerful Jin Empire demanded the Kerait tribe pay their **tribute**. The Kerait were now part of the Mongol state. Genghis Khan invaded the Jin, despite their army of a million men. After every defeat the Jin still raised new armies. The war was still going on when Genghis Khan died!

A Mongol coin

In 1211, a civil war began between the **Kara Khitai** ruler, Yelü Zhilugu and his son-in-law, Kuchlug. Genghis Khan decided to take the side of Zhilugu and sent an army. By the time his army arrived, Zhilugu had died. Genghis Khan defeated Kuchlug and forced the surviving Kara Khitai soldiers to join his army.

In August 1227, Genghis Khan died suddenly while on a campaign in western China. Some say he was killed by an arrow, others that he fell from his horse, or was stabbed by a captive princess. Nobody knows the truth. His body was taken back to Mongolia by an escort of several thousand men. To keep his burial site secret, the Mongols killed everyone they met on the journey! He was buried near the mountain where he was born. Nobody knows where the grave is.

A statue of Genghis Khan

Discipline

The Mongol state was ready for war. The **nomad** tribes had fought each other in feuds and conflicts, so the men were skilled in fighting and tactics. Once the tribes were united under Genghis Khan those skills were ruthlessly directed toward the conquest of other peoples and states.

When Genghis Khan united the nomadic tribes, he took care to reform their society. He was determined that never again would nomad fight nomad. He broke up the power the chiefs had over their people so that no leader could start a rebellion or uprising. The Merkit, Oirat, Khalka and others were absorbed into the Mongol state and became one people.

A nomadic Mongol tribe's traditional home, the ger, is easy to transport.

The Mongols believed men should be promoted because of their worth, not simply if they came from a noble family. This was important in wartime when the best commanders were needed.

The Mongols had a set of unwritten laws known as the Yassa which were memorized by chiefs and priests. The Yassa was not just a law code, but also included religious duties, **philosophical** views and **mystical** chants.

ALL RELIGIONS WELCOME

Mongol tribes practised several different religions including Christianity, Islam, Buddhism and Shamanism. When Genghis Khan united the tribes he let any Mongol practise whatever religion they liked.

Tough penalties

Because the Mongols were nomads, any punishments handed out for crimes had to be swift and easy to impose. Among the penalties were:

Crime	Penalty
Proclaim a person to be khan	Death
Steal from an enemy	Death
Cut the throat of a **yak**	Death
Steal a horse	Death
Give clothes to a slave	Death
Wash clothes during a thunderstorm	Whipping
Drink water from cupped hands	Whipping
Refuse to share food with a stranger	Whipping

a yak

Mongol recruitment

Every Mongol man was a warrior. Mongol society was harsh and violent, so there was no room for a man who could not use a bow, sword or lance.

The Mongols lived on the windy open grasslands of central Asia. There are virtually no trees. The soil is too poor to grow crops, and few crops could survive the long, bitterly cold winters. Most Mongolians survived by raising what are known as the five muzzles; cattle, sheep, goats, horses and camels.

WARRIOR FOOD

Mongolians ate mostly meat or dairy products. Milk was drunk, or used to make cheese, yogurt or **kumis**. Kumis was a drink made of fermented mare's milk. It had an alcohol content similar to a weak beer. Mongol warriors drank kumis to celebrate a success. Horsemeat was thought the tastiest and best, but most people ate sheep or goats.

Although every male Mongol was expected to be a warrior, he did not serve in the army full time. Men would herd their livestock and care for their families. When a tribe went to war the chief would decide which men would join him on campaign. Nobody was allowed to refuse to go, or they would be killed.

Every Mongol owned several different horses. Some were for riding, some for giving milk, others for breeding, and a few were eaten. The horses lived outside all year and had to be tough to survive the bitter winter. They were stocky and strong, with enormous **stamina**. They could gallop for hours without a break.

That's fearless!

In 1241, a Mongol army led by Batu Khan invaded Hungary. Batu wanted to catch the Hungarian army before it was ready to fight. He led the Mongol horsemen on a ride of 1,000 km taking just 8 days. They crushed the Hungarians, killing over 30,000 of them!

Mongols were expected to be able to ride a horse from as young as three years old. A family might have to move to fresh pastures or water supplies at short notice. The fact that Mongols spent hours in the saddle every day from a young age made them superb horsemen.

13

Training For War

Mongol warriors trained constantly for war. They were ferociously skilled with their weapons, as well as with their tactics and strategies. To make sure that they stuck to their training, the Mongols used the most brutally effective discipline of any army in history.

Mongolian armies were organised by groups of ten. Ten men made up an **arban**, ten arban made up a **zuun** of 100 men, ten zuun made up a **mingghan** numbering 1,000 men and ten Mingghan made up a **turmen** of 10,000 men. Each commander was responsible for the ten men under him. The leader of a turmen commanded just the ten Mingghan commanders, not every man in his turmen. Each man was free to carry out his orders as he saw fit. Mongol commanders concentrated on the big issues. They left the small details to their juniors.

That's fearless!

A commander's orders could be harsh. General Subutai instructed his men that one of the straps holding their horses' saddles should be kept loose on a march to stop riders going too fast and wearing out their horses. He told his officers "Any man who ignores this decree, cut off his head where he stands."

Mongol khans had a personal bodyguard called the **kheshig**, which means 'blessed ones'. Genghis Khan had a kheshig of 120 men and 32 officers, each of whom had sworn eternal loyalty until death. The unit was split into a day watch and a night watch, with each man spending three days on duty, then three days off. This meant that wherever he went Genghis Khan always had 38 alert guards beside him.

A modern-day Mongolian bokh competition

WRESTLING

The Mongols used **bokh**, or wrestling, as a way to keep fit and train men for war. The winner is the first man to force his opponent to touch the ground with any part of his body other than his foot. Each bout is begun with a dance in which the wrestler imitates an animal. Fights could be dangerous and more than one warrior was killed in a wrestling match.

Battle tactics

City sieges

As the Mongols lived on open plains with no cities or fortresses, at first they had no experience of how to attack city walls.

When the Mongols conquered the Kara Khitan Empire they forced Khitan soldiers to join their army. The Khitan army's **siege** engineers knew how to build weapons that could throw heavy boulders or fire large bolts to smash city walls. The Mongols learned a great deal from their new recruits.

TREBUCHET

The Mongol's most powerful siege weapon worked by a lever action. A wooden container filled with stones was dropped onto one side of the trebuchet's lever. The weight lifted the opposite side of the lever and hurled whatever was on it with great force. Large trebuchets could throw heavy boulders over walls to destroy houses, food stores or people!

TOILET HABITS

The Mongols went to the bathroom wherever they liked. They were usually on the move in small groups, so there was little danger of disease. When thousands of Mongols camped close together for weeks during a siege, diseases spread rapidly. One of the most important siege skills the Khitan taught the Mongols was the importance of digging **latrines**!

CATAPULT

The catapult used the tension of twisted animal sinews to propel any item placed in its large cup. Stones or boulders could be hurled forwards with great power to smash into defensive walls.

KHARASH

One brutal tactic the Mongols used during a siege was the kharash. When they were ready to launch an attack on a broken section of wall the Mongols would gather local people or captured soldiers. They were pushed forward at sword point to form a human shield for the Mongols to follow behind. Any arrows shot by the city under attack would kill their own townspeople and leave the Mongols unharmed.

A Mongol siege, using trebuchets

Horsepower

Horse archers

About 60 per cent of any Mongol army was made up of horse archers. These men were armed with bows and arrows and swords. They rode without armour so that they could ride fast and turn quickly.

The Mongol bow was a weapon used by all the nomadic tribes of Asia. It was made of several layers of sinew, wood and horn glued together and then bound in birchbark or leather. The bow was small and powerful. Its short length of around 1 m meant that the archer could switch direction from one side of the horse to the other with ease.

Most arrows were made of birch rods. The flights were made from the tail feathers of large birds, usually cranes. Flights make the arrows spin in the air and keep them accurate. The arrowheads were usually made of iron and were triangular in shape. Occasionally small whistles were fitted to the arrowhead so that the flying arrow made a terrifying screaming noise.

A key skill of horse archers was the ability to shoot accurately backwards over the horse's tail while riding at a gallop. This allowed them to shoot at the enemy even when retreating at top speed.

That's fearless!

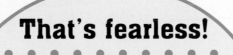

Horse archers wore silk underwear as their only protection in battle. If hit by an arrow, the silk was dragged into the wound and, when pulled gently, would tease out the arrow.

BATTLE BEGINS

A Mongol commander would start a battle by sending in his horse archers. They galloped forward showering the enemy with arrows, and then galloped away before the enemy could respond. A series of these attacks would cause many enemy casualties at little cost to the Mongols.

Mounted lancers

There were only about half as many mounted lancers in a Mongol army as there were horse archers, but it was the lancers who were the real killers. Victory depended on the discipline, aggression and skill of the lancers.

The lancers wore tough armour made from dozens of small plates of iron. The plates were laced together to form a long jacket that reached from the neck down to the knees and forearms. This method of construction produced armour that was light, easy to maintain and flexible. Some horsemen preferred armour of toughened leather, which was even lighter.

That's fearless!

When Genghis Khan was wounded in a battle his friend Jelme crept into the enemy camp at night to steal a tub of yoghurt. The yoghurt revived Genghis Khan enough to allow him to mount his horse and escape.

Mongol helmets were usually made of iron or toughened leather. They were sometimes lined with fur to keep the wearer warm on winter campaigns. The helmet was usually in the shape of a point, with flaps that hung down to protect the cheeks and the back of the neck.

The Mongolian lance was about 3 m long and was made of bamboo or wood topped by an iron tip. The lancers always carried a second weapon in case the lance snapped. Curved **scimitars** were the usual sidearm, but some men preferred axes or straight swords.

IN BATTLE

In battle the lancers were usually held back at the start. Only after the archers had inflicted many casualties or disrupted the enemy formation would the lancers be ordered to charge in and finish the battle.

A Chinese scimitar

21

Mongol horses

The key to Mongol success was the Mongolian horse. This unique breed is still used by the Mongolians for herding livestock and transport and for sport. In the hands of the Mongol armies, the horse allowed them to travel further, faster and more efficiently than any other army on Earth.

The **Aduu**, or Mongolian horse, is a short, stocky, muscular horse that has a larger head than most breeds. The hair, mane and tail are all long and shaggy, which helps the horses survive the Mongolian winter.

It is thought that the climate of Central Asia between about 1100 and 1300 was warmer and wetter than it is today. The grass grew well and provided better food for the horses. This good grazing helped the Mongol armies cover great distances and create larger armies than they could before.

A favourite food of the Mongols on campaign was **borts**. This is yak meat that is cut into strips and dried in cool, circulating air – usually inside a ger in the autumn or winter. The meat is then pounded into a powder and stored in bags for months or years. When needed the borts is boiled in water to make soup.

A yak is a type of long-haired cattle.

SPARE HORSES

Mongol warriors took five or six horses each on campaign. They could change horses if one became tired during a long journey. When going into battle the Mongols always changed to a fresh horse. Some men kept one horse for use only in battle.

That's fearless!

Mongols carried food with them on a pack horse. If they had to move very fast the food had to be left behind. The men would drink the milk of their own horses. If they got really hungry, they would slit a vein in the horse's neck and drink their blood! Sometimes a horse would be killed and eaten.

Sons of Genghis Khan

Genghis Khan had four sons, Jochi, Chagatai, Ögedei and Tolui. Even though Jochi was the eldest, Ghenghis passed his throne on to his third son, Ögedei.

Genghis Khan's third son, Ögedei

Jochi

When Jochi was 26 years old, Genghis Khan gave him command of a campaign against the Kyrgyz peoples. He won. During the invasion of the Khwarzmian Empire, Jochi argued with his brother Chagatei. Genghis Khan put Ögedei in charge as punishment.

Chagatai

Second son Chagatai's argument with Jochi caused a split in the family. Chagatai fought with his father against the Jin and the Khwarzmian Empire, but was rarely trusted with a command. He refused to live in a town and lived as a nomad wandering the grasslands. When he died in 1241 his sons were already dead, so his kingdom went to his grandson, Qara Hülëgü.

Modern nomads

Ögedei

When Genghis Khan's third son was 17 years old he was badly wounded in battle against his father's rival Jamukha. Ögedei was left unconscious on the battlefield and everyone thought he was dead until a friend rescued him. His first command was a two-year raid deep into Jin territory. Ögedei was the most ruthless of Genghis Khan's sons, ordering large massacres and slaughters. He sent armies to conquer Persia (now Iran), Afghanistan, northwestern India, Armenia, Georgia and Korea. He started the invasions of China's Song Empire and Europe, too. He died suddenly after a late-night party!

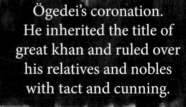

Ögedei's coronation. He inherited the title of great khan and ruled over his relatives and nobles with tact and cunning.

That's fearless!

• • • • • • • • • • •

In 1229 Ögedei fell dangerously ill on campaign. The chief shaman said it was due to the hostile water spirits of China. Tolui grabbed a cup of water and declared that he took all the evil on himself. He drank, choked and died. Within hours Ögedei was better.

Tolui

The youngest son first went into combat in wars against the Jin. He led the assault on the walled city of Dexing by climbing the first ladder himself! He showed himself to be talented and ruthless, ordering the massacres at Merv and Nishapur (see page 27). He led campaigns into China to conquer new areas for Ögedei.

Battle tactics

Terror

The Mongols used terror as a weapon. They used cruelty to demoralise their enemies and to make them run away or surrender. The most terrifying of all the Mongol campaigns was the total destruction of the Khwarazmian Empire.

DON'T ANNOY GENGHIS!

In 1218, Genghis Khan asked to trade with the Khwarzmian Empire. Its ruler, Shah Ala ad-Din Muhammad thought it was a trick to invade his land and would not agree. Genghis sent a small party to Khwarzm to ask again. A governor accused the party of spying and arrested them. To maintain diplomacy, Genghis sent an envoy of three men to ask the Shah to hand over the governor to the Mongols for punishment. The shah executed the envoy! Genghis Khan's revenge was brutal, even by Mongol standards. Shah Ala ad-Din Muhammad fled before the Mongol armies arrived. He sailed around the Caspian Sea in disguise and hid on a small island, where he fell ill and died.

A huge statue of Genghis Khan in the Mongolian capital of Ulan Batur

BUKHARA 1220

In 1220, Genghis Khan led an army across the barren desert of Kyzyl Kum in Central Asia to attack the city of Bukhara. The defending **garrison** had thought that it was impossible for an army to cross the desert and had been watching the other roads. Taken entirely by surprise, the garrison surrendered. The officers of the garrison were killed, while the rest of the garrison and the entire civilian population was sold into slavery.

The walls of Bukhara

URGENCH 1221

Urgench was the wealthiest city in the Khwarazmian Empire. The Mongols attacked in 1221. After several weeks, they broke into the city and killed the entire garrison. The people were ordered to leave the city and line up on the plain outside with whatever household goods they could carry. A group of 500 skilled craftsmen was marched away to slavery in Mongolia. Everyone else was then killed. The heads of more than a million dead were made into a gruesome artificial hill to warn others of the fate of those who opposed Genghis Khan!

MERV 1221

After the destruction of Urgench, many fled to the apparently invincible walled city of Merv. When a Mongol army under Tolui arrived the governor of Merv asked to surrender. Tolui said that the civilians and garrison could walk free, but that they could take only the clothes they were wearing. The city surrendered and the people walked out, leaving their property behind. Tolui then ordered his men to shoot everyone dead with arrows. Nobody knows how many died, but it was probably over half a million!

Mongol strategy

Mongol strategy aimed for the total and utter destruction of the enemy. They were not interested in peace treaties. Instead they only counted a victory when the enemy had been wiped out or forced to surrender.

Before invading, the Mongols would investigate enemy territory. They sent men disguised as merchants or holy men to draw maps of the roads, discover good pasture and find where reliable water sources were. This sometimes took years. Before an attack they would sometimes make offers of friendship to persuade the enemy that no war was likely. As soon as the enemy relaxed, the Mongols attacked.

DISTRACTIONS

When attacking one country, the Mongols would make smaller raids into neighbouring states. This stopped them sending armies to help their allies.

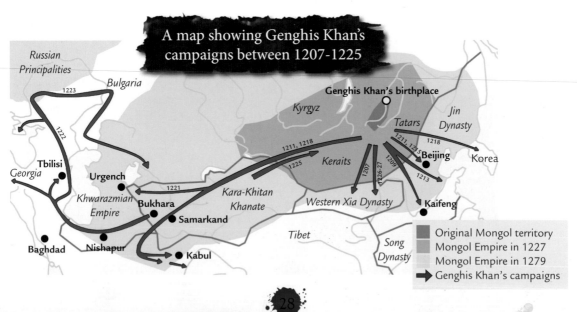

A map showing Genghis Khan's campaigns between 1207-1225

Russian Principalities

Bulgaria

Genghis Khan's birthplace

Kyrgyz

Jin Dynasty

Tatars

1223

1222

Tbilisi
Georgia

Urgench

1211, 1218

Keraits

1225

1211, 1215
1218

Beijing

Korea

1221

Khwarazmian Empire

Bukhara

Kara-Khitan Khanate

1207

1226-27

1209

1213

Samarkand

Western Xia Dynasty

Kaifeng

Baghdad

Nishapur

Kabul

Tibet

Song Dynasty

Original Mongol territory
Mongol Empire in 1227
Mongol Empire in 1279
Genghis Khan's campaigns

Groups of horse archers would be sent to launch attacks many miles away from the main army. Their job was to attack but allow some people to escape. These people reported back that Mongol horsemen were in the area, confusing the enemy commander as to where the main Mongol army actually was.

TRIBUTES

When the Mongols did not have the resources to attack a rival power they would send envoys asking for payments instead. The alternative to paying these tributes was invasion and destruction. The Mongol reputation meant that people paid up. Korea paid 10,000 otter skins, 20,000 horses, 10,000 bolts of silk, clothing for 1,000,000 soldiers and 1,000 children as slaves every year!

That's fearless!

When Genghis Khan invaded the Jin State of northern China he had several aims. He wanted to steal its wealth, capture slaves to work for the Mongols and gain good new pasture for his horses. Whenever he found an area of good pasture, he ordered that all the local farmers and their families be slaughtered so that the land would be empty for the use of Mongol horses.

Battle tactics

Doomed cities

The Mongols were nomads who despised people who lived in cities. Other conquerors might keep a captured city intact and tax its people. The Mongols simply stole everything and killed everyone.

KAIFENG 1232

Ögedei Khan sent his commander Subutai and about 50,000 men to lay siege to Kaifeng, the capital city of the Jin State. Kaifeng's defence was led by Emperor Aizong with about 140,000 men. Gunpowder weapons were used in large amounts for the first time. The Jin catapulted pots of gunpowder at the Mongols, killing anyone nearby. The Jin also used an early type of flame thrower. After nine months, Emperor Aizong and his advisors slipped out of the city, leaving commander Cui Li in charge. Cui Li contacted Subutai and offered to change sides! Subutai agreed. The people had to hand over their valuables, but the city and the people were unharmed.

An ancient Chinese drawing of Subutai

NISHAPUR 1221

Nishapur had a population of about 700,000 when Tokuchar, son-in-law of Genghis Khan arrived and demanded surrender. The city refused. In the following battle Tokuchar was killed. Tolui arrived and captured the city in three days. Tokuchar's widow told Tolui to kill everyone. Then she ordered him to kill all the dogs and cats, and burn every building!

BAGHDAD 1258

When the Caliph of Abassid refused to pay tribute to the Mongol Empire, Möngke Khan sent his brother Hulagu to the capital, Baghdad. The Caliph sent out an ambassador, but Hulagu refused to see him. 3,000 leading citizens went to talk to the Mongols. Hulagu killed them all! After 12 days the Mongols broke through the city walls. The Caliph surrendered and was killed. Hulagu's men stole valuables, enslaved anyone useful and killed everyone else. About 500,000 were killed and the city burned to the ground. Important Islamic writings were lost when the library burned.

An ancient illustration showing the conquest of Baghdad

Great commanders

The Mongol campaigns took place over a vast area. Dozens of commanders led armies to distant battles. Here are some of the greatest.

SUBUTAI

The son of a poor blacksmith, Subutai joined Genghis Khan as a soldier. He was rapidly promoted. His first victory was over the Merkit. He led an army on a fast campaign to ride right around the Caspian Sea! Subutai finished the campaign against the Jin State, and invaded the Song Empire.

YELÜ CHUCAI

Yelü Chucai was an adviser to Genghis Khan. He was the first Mongol government official who could read and write! He showed Genghis Khan that written records were more reliable than memory. When Ögedei mocked him for being a bad horserider, Yelü Chucai replied "You can conquer an empire on horseback, but you cannot govern it from horseback."

This satellite image of the Caspian Sea shows how large an area Subutai's fast campaign covered.

That's fearless!

At the age of 70 Subutai organized an invasion of Song China, but sensibly said he was too old to lead the invasion himself!

A painting showing the battle between Kublai Khan and the Tatars

KUBLAI KHAN

Kublai was the son of Tolui. After the death of Möngke Khan a civil war between the Mongols led to Kublai becoming leader. He completed the conquest of the Song Dynasty, giving him control over China, Korea and Mongolia. He declared himself Emperor of China, and abandoned the Mongolian way of life.

MUQALI

Muqali was a slave. He became a trusted supporter of Genghis Khan. When Genghis invaded the Khwarazmian Empire, he left Muqali with 20,000 men to guard the border with the Jin. Muqali decided to attack instead. He defeated the Jin in 12 battles. On his deathbed he sent a message to Genghis Khan – "Tell him I have never been defeated."

BATU

Batu was the son of Jochi. He commanded the Mongol invasion of the Rus with Subutai. He captured the great city of Ryazan and won the Battle of the Sit River. He destroyed 14 more cities and captured the Crimea.

Battle tactics

Pretend retreats

The most famous tactic used by Mongol armies was the feigned retreat. The Mongols pretended to run away to lure the enemy into a trap.

Sometimes the Mongols would retreat for days before the trap was sprung, other times the wait would be for only a few minutes. The Mongols could use this tactic as their commanders knew that the strict discipline of the Mongol armies meant a pretend retreat would not turn into a real one.

KALKA RIVER 1223

Mstislav the Bold of Galich and Mstislav III of Kiev defeated a small force of Mongols. When the main Mongol army retreated Mstislav the Bold gave chase, thinking he had forced Subutai to flee. Subutai retreated for nine days until Mstislav's army became disordered, then he attacked. The Mongol horse archers surrounded them, while the heavily armoured lancers charged each small unit in turn and wiped them out. Subutai had Msitislav of Kiev buried alive and held a victory feast over his grave.

Mstislav the Bold on a monument in Novgorod, Russia

MOHI 1241

The Mongols led by Batu Khan invaded Hungary. King Bela IV mustered an army inside a fort at Mohi. A force of Mongols was spotted robbing nearby villages. The Hungarians defeated them and celebrated. At dawn a Mongol force of 20,000 men stormed over the river, catching the Hungarians by surprise. The terrified Hungarians fled through a gap deliberately left in the lines. Once the Hungarian army had left, the Mongols attacked the fort! King Bela escaped and rode all the way to the Mediterranean before the Mongols gave up the chase!

SAMARKAND 1220

Samarkand had strong walls and a garrison of 100,000 men. Genghis Khan laid siege. After three days the Mongols pretended to retreat and the garrison rushed out to attack them. It was a trap. In a counter-attack they wiped out most of the garrison. The city surrendered. Genghis Khan ordered the execution of all the remaining soldiers. Everyone who wasn't useful to the Mongols was killed. It is thought that 250,000 people died.

LIEGNITZ 1241

A force of 20,000 Mongols under Kadan invaded Poland. King Henry II of Poland, with 25,000 men, ambushed the advance guard of the Mongol army. The Mongols fled toward their main army. Kadan ordered his men to set fire to the dry grass around Liegnitz, causing vast clouds of smoke. Henry lost sight of the Mongols, but they were bringing up their main force behind the smoke. Kadan launched a devastating attack that killed Henry and most of his men.

Mongol queens

In Mongol society women were in control of the home. When a man was away herding livestock on distant pastures he would leave his wife in charge of the home and the family. Genghis Khan continued this tradition by appointing his wife Börte to rule in his absence.

Genghis Khan family tree

Genghis Khan m Börte

Sons					Daughters	
Jochi	Chagadai	**Ögodei** m Töregene	Tolui m Sorghaghtani		Checheikhen	Alakhai
Batu		**Güyük** Qashi	**Möngke** **Kublai** Ariq			

m = married
names in **bold** = khans

Töregene Khatun

Töregene married Qudu of the Merkit. When Genghis Khan conquered the Merkit he chose the widowed Töregene to marry his son Ögedei. On his death the Mongol nobles chose Töregene to be in charge until the Mongol chiefs chose the next khan. She then declared war on the Song Dynasty! Töregene kept delaying the chiefs' meeting until she was sure most would vote her son Güyük to be khan! Güyük became khan in 1246.

Checeikhen

Genghis Khan demanded that the Oirat of the Altai Mountains join his state and their warriors join his army. Instead they offered the marriage of their King Qutuqi Beki to Genghis Khan's daughter Checeikhen. Genghis Khan agreed, then instructed Qutuqi Beki to join his army. That left his daughter in control of the Altai region! Checeikhen ruled the territory until her death.

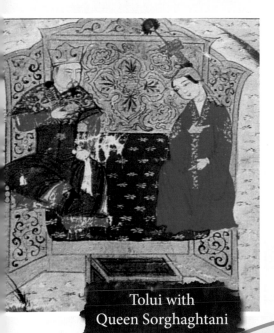

Tolui with Queen Sorghaghtani

Sorghaghtani Beki

Sorghaghtani married Genghis' son Tolui. Güyük Khan, her nephew, died suddenly, probably murdered on the orders of Sorghaghtani who wanted her son Möngke to be khan! Sorghaghtani reformed the Mongol Empire. She introduced written government records to replace spoken instructions. She encouraged trade, gaining more wealth through taxes than by invading and robbing other countries.

That's fearless!

Alakhai was Genghis Khan's daughter. She married the eldest son of the ruler of the Ongud tribe. After Alakhai became co-ruler with her husband, he was killed in a rebellion. Alakhai fled to her father, who put her in command of an army to seek revenge. Alakhai crushed the rebels and executed her enemies. She led the Ongud troops until her death in the 1240s.

Mongol tactics

Surprise attacks

An attack when the enemy is not expecting it is more likely to succeed than if the enemy is ready. The Mongols went to great lengths to disguise where or when they were likely to attack.

SIT RIVER 1238

The army of Batu Khan led by the Burundei invaded the collection of small states known as the Rus, later to become Russia. Grand Duke Yuri II of Vladimir, Prince Vsevolod of Yaroslavl and Duke Dorozh with about 15,000 men gathered on the banks of the River Sit. Under cover of darkness the Mongols surrounded their camp and at dawn launched a surprise attack. Before dusk had fallen the entire Rus army had been wiped out.

A statue of a rider chasing along the Mongolian grasslands

WADI AL-KHAZANDAR

The Mongols attacked Egypt in 1299. Ghazan Khan led an army of 100,000 Mongols and 60,000 allies. At Wadi al-Khazandar, Ghazan was met by 40,000 Egyptians under Al-Nasir Muhammad. At dawn the Egyptians attacked the Mongol camp, surprising the Mongols before they could find their bows. After hours of fighting, the right flank of the Egyptian army broke and fled, followed by the rest of the army.

Wadi al-Khazandar

That's fearless!

The Mongol forces would sometimes chase their fleeing enemy for long distances. After the battle at Wadi al-Khazandar the Mongols chased the Egyptians for over 200 km killing every soldier they could find.

BADGER PASS

In 1211, Genghis Khan led 80,000 Mongols to attack the State of Jin. Prince Shao and his army met the Mongol advance at Badger Pass. He put 300,000 **infantry** in the pass and held his 150,000 **cavalry** back as a reserve. Genghis Khan studied the landscape, then sent half his army over the mountains, where the Jin thought no horses could survive. Genghis Khan launched a pretend attack on the pass. His soldiers on the mountains attacked the resting Jin cavalry. They then attacked the rear of the Jin infantry in the pass. Attacked on both sides the Jin infantry fled. They were hunted down by the Mongols. The Jin lost about 300,000 men. The Mongols lost less than 5,000.

Mongol timeline

1162
Probable date of the birth of Temujin, later to be Genghis Khan.

1160

1177
Temujin is captured and enslaved by the Tayichi'ud. He then escapes and begins to build up a following of warriors.

1188
The kidnap of Börte, wife of Temujin, by the Merkit tribe leads to Temujin's defeat of the Merkits and his rise to become chief of the Mongols.

1190

1206
After a series of wars, Temujin is recognised as supreme ruler (Genghis Khan) of the Mongols, Naiman, Merkit, Tangut and Tatar tribes of nomads. He unites the tribes into a single nation: the Mongols.

That's fearless!

The warrior Chilaun was paying a visit to the Tayichi'ud tribe when he recognized a man kept as a slave. It was Temujin, later Genghis Khan. That night Chilaun released Temujin and escaped with him. The Tayichi'ud chased the pair for days.

1211
Genghis Khan invades the Jin State of northern China. By 1215 the Jin were defeated and driven out of the north of their empire.

1219
Genghis Khan invades the Khwarazmian Empire after his envoy is executed. The campaign ends in victory and utter devastation for the Khwarazmian Empire. Around 90 per cent of the population is killed.

1230

1210

1218
Genghis Khan invades the Khitan Empire. The empire is conquered in less than a year.

1220
First Mongol invasion of Europe. Jebe and Subutai lead a raid through Armenia, Georgia and the Rus.

1227
Death of Genghis Khan. His son Ögedei becomes great khan.

1232
Ögedei renews the war against the Jin and within three years has completely destroyed them.

1238
Ögedei launches an invasion of Song China.

1241
Ögedei's death is followed by the regency of Töregene until 1246 when Güyük is chosen as next great khan.

1230

1240

1237
Jochi's son Batu Khan leads the Mongol invasion of Russia, which is completed by 1240.

1240
Ögedei orders raids into northern India, resulting in the conquest of Afghanistan and Kashmir.

1241
Mongol invasion of Europe results in the conquest of Hungary and raids into Poland and Austria.

Kazakh hunters in the Mongol Empire would hunt using eagles.

A model of the Mongol palace at Karakorum. Möngke Khan had the palace enlarged.

1248
Death of Güyük, Möngke becomes the next great khan.

1254
Möngke renews war against the Song.

1259
Death of Möngke. After a civil war, Kublai becomes great khan, but never achieves full control of the Mongol Empire. The Empire divides into smaller states, often at war with each other.

1250

1253
Conquest of the Dali Kingdom in southwestern China.

1256
Möngke invades the Abbasid Caliphate, resulting in the destruction of Baghdad, and conquest of Syria and Palestine.

1300

1294
Death of Kublai Khan. The Mongol Empire divides into the Yuan (China and Mongolia), Ilkhan (Persia, Iraq and Afghanistan), Chagatai (Central Asia) and Golden Horde (Russia and lands northeast of the Caspian Sea).

That's fearless!

Wounds were treated by being pulled apart so that yoghurt could be poured in, and then sucked out by mouth! It was believed this stopped infections.

What do you know?

Can you answer these questions about the Mongols?

1. How was a Mongol bow made?

2. What is bort?

3. What did Mongol warriors wear under their armour?

4. When did Genghis Khan die?

5. What was a kheshig?

6. Who succeeded Genghis Khan as the ruler of the Mongols?

7. What was a mingghan?

8. How old was a Mongol when he was taught to ride?

9. What is the name for the Mongolian breed of horse?

10. What was Genghis Khan's name?

Answers on page 48

Further information

Books

Roux, Jean-Paul. *Genghis Khan and the Mongol Empire*. Thames & Hudson, 2003.

Turnbull, Stephen. *Mongol Warrior*. Osprey Publishing, 2003.

Turnbull, Stephen. *Genghis Khan and the Mongol Conquests 1190-1400*. Osprey Publishing, 2003.

Websites

Facts about Genghis Khan
http://www.history.com/topics/genghis-khan

Biography of Genghis Khan
http://www.biography.com/people/genghis-khan-9308634#synopsis

Animated map of the growth of the Mongol Empire
https://www.youtube.com/watch?v=v_NPgMMazF4

Glossary

Aduu The Mongolian breed of horse.

allies Countries that fight alongside one another against a common enemy.

arban A unit of 10 men in the Mongol army.

bokh A form of wrestling popular in Mongolia.

borts A popular Mongolian food made of dried yak meat.

cavalry Men who fight on horseback.

envoy A person sent to carry a message from one ruler to another.

garrison A military post.

infantry Men who fight on foot.

Jin State A state covering most of north and northeast China that was ruled by nobles from the Jurgen people. It was founded in 1115.

Kara Khitai A Christian state in cesntral Asia organised on Chinese lines that covered a large area east of the Aral Sea.

kheshig Royal bodyguard.

Khwarazmian Empire An Islamic state covering modern Iran, plus parts of Afghanistan, Uzbekistan and Turkmenistan. It was founded in 1077.

kumis An alcoholic drink made from mare's milk.

latrines Temporary toilets made by digging a hole in the ground.

mingghan A unit of 1000 men in the Mongol army.

mystical Efforts to communicate with gods or spirits through secret rituals or meditation.

nomad A lifestyle that involves constantly moving around looking for fresh sources of food.

philosophical The pursuit of wisdom or knowledge through thought and contemplation.

scimitars Sword with a long, curved blade.

siege A military campaign in which one army shelters behind strong fortifications, while the other tries to break through the defences. Sieges often involve attacks on towns or cities.

stamina The ability to continue working or travelling for long periods of time without resting.

Tatars A nomadic people who lived in Eastern Europe and who spoke a language similar to Turkish. Their descendants today inhabit lands north and east of the Caspian Sea.

tribute A payment in money or objects made by one ruler to another as a form of tax.

turmen A unit of 10,000 men in the Mongol army.

Xi Xia Empire A state in northwestern China that was ruled by nobles from the Tangut people. It was founded in 982.

yak A type of cattle native to Mongolia.

zuun A unit of 100 men in the Mongol army.

Index

Answers to Quiz

1. layers of sinew, wood and horn
    glued together and bound in
    birchbark or leather
2. powder made from dried
    yak's meat
3. silk underwear
4. 1227
5. the royal bodyguard
6. Ögedei
7. a unit of 10,000 men
8. 3 years old
9. Aduu
10. Temujin